How Literally Anyone Can Become A Millionaire

Your Proven Formula for Millionaire Success

By Strive for 25
With Joel Farrell

Table of Contents

Preface

This book is all about helping the average person build wealth and become financially successful so that they can live with the power of choice and pursue the life of their dreams.

However, we have to lay the foundation before we can build the house. We must have the right software to be able to use the hardware. Could you imagine running your IPhone 14 on IOS 3? It wouldn't work.

This means we have to establish the right set of assumptions and context before we can be in the right mindset to offer solutions on how to take you from your current situation to the next level.

These strategies, insights and series of stories can be implemented immediately. Once you decide to go all-in, you will be well on your way to making your goals and dreams come true!

Introduction

There is power in printed word. Let's face it, we receive so much more than mental exercise when we are reading. Throughout my life, I have received gifts in the form of written word, that at the time, I didn't even realize how impactful they were. In fact, the book that set me on a course of narrowing down the teachings of Strive for 25 was one called *The Power of Consistency*, by Weldon Long.

I read the book back in 2018, and it is essentially about the author being in jail three different times. He had a child he had never seen, and the child's mother ended up in jail. He was in a pretty bad spot, had no hope, nothing going for him, and then in 1996 his father passed away. At the darkest point in his life, something just clicked inside him. At that time, he still had a few years left on his sentence in jail, he realize that he had to get it together. He dug into different books, the Tony Robbins books, the Stephen Covey books, and he started to realize that the circumstances he was currently in was not anyone else's fault, it was a consequence of his own choices and actions.

These authors demonstrated through their words, that your thoughts literally dictate your results. Your thoughts affect your emotions and your emotions affect your actions and then over time, your actions affect your results.

He started to realize that he actually did have control over the results. If you're putting positive thoughts into your brain, you're going to lead to positive results. If you're putting a positive thought into your brain, and our brains can only think about one thing at a time, then by default, that positive thought is not a negative, right?

This rings true in every aspect in our lives. When you're having negative finances, the average person goes out and gets a second job. For Weldon Long, he decided to rob banks. When he had this mental awakening, he changed the way he thought, and you guessed it, his results changed.

Reading through his book, it hit me. I've accomplished a lot in my journey in the mortgage industry. I've been #1 in my company a couple different times, and at the same time was slowly building a real estate portfolio and seeing some successes. At the same time, I wasn't fulfilled. I wasn't where I wanted to be. I knew I could do more. I knew I could help more people.

That was the catalyst for me. I started taking these principles and putting them into action. In the book, Weldon Long talks about his coined term, "Prosperity Plan" where you put your vision and your goal and a couple of action items out there and it's something you review every single day. So if you are reviewing your vision, goals, and action items every day, you will either make it a reality or you will stop reviewing it, there is no other option. That's because your brain does not like being lied to.

I knew that I wanted to build our team and do more business, so that I could have the luxury to be able to spend more time on this Strive for 25 project that was in my head... I knew that there was only one choice for me. That I had to keep marching toward this dream of making Strive something tangible. When you talk about power, is there more power in running toward something or running away from something?

For me, I was more running from something... the fear and anxiety of being complacent.

I wasn't sure how I was going to get there, I just knew I wanted to get there. I started looking at my vision and goal every day...every single day, and I did not stop.

Fast forward, growth continued to happen in the mortgage industry, we continued to build our team, I continued to build my real estate portfolio, and then things started to kick into another gear.

In 2022, Strive 25 was still just a thought. I had a couple of talks in front of crowds, a couple of presentations, but nothing in terms of a platform. The mortgage industry was hitting some tough times in 2022 with the market shifting and I knew that what I was doing before wasn't going to be enough. I knew I had to figure out how to do business differently.

From a social media standpoint, I knew that I wanted to take the time to really dig into building Strive 25. I began building and fleshing out all of the social media for Strive 25, with 2 ½ year old twin boys! The amount of time I had within a day was limited. I'm sure you know that feeling.

But I had to go through some rough patches. The time I spent on this platform was after hours. My typical day includes getting up with our boys, getting them off to school, work, and then by 5 taking over again for the boys because my wife is still seeing clients at that time. Then dinner, bath, and night time routine means I wouldn't be done until around 8 pm. And by that time I'm exhausted.   The stress and anxiety of having to ramp back up and get some work done was crushing me. Some days on some days off,

I knew I had to take the principles I had read about and really apply them. In the book Atomic Habits, James Clear talks about the process of building habits, and how missing a day breaks the chain.   Two minutes of work is enough to keep it going.

At that point, I was all in, and I started implementing my own version of the 2-minute rule. I would log in every night after getting the boys to bed. Even on the days that I didn't want to do it, or I felt like crap, I made myself do at least the two minutes.

I would set a for two minutes the first few times, and at first, it was extremely uncomfortable stopping after two minutes. But that's what I did.

And a few days of that, I started ramping up and doing more. Within a 2 weeks, I started looking forward to getting some work done. I had trained my mind to love the process.

Today, I'm continuing to train my subconscious to reach my goals. Our social media platforms are continuing to grow, and we're putting out content constantly, and building community!

We both know you're not reading this book just to hear about some things I've done. You're reading this book to find your own success, or maybe to answer some questions for yourself and figure out how to reach your goals financially. You're looking for results. I want you to have them. I want you to gain financial fortitude so that you can build wealth and live your life every single day with the power of choice. So let's do that. Let's dive in and get those written tools for you to implement. My hope is that this book is the catalyst for your financial fortitude and that the written word can change your life like it did for me.

Chapter One: Power of Choice

<u>What Are We Drawn To?</u>

I have been in the mortgage industry since 2006, and have had some success in building business over the years. I got into real estate investing in 2013 when I purchased my second home, and turned the old one into a rental.

I didn't really have a mentor from a real estate investing standpoint at that time. It wasn't until 2019 that I really started to see the fruits of my labor. In 2017 I purchased a couple of 4 family units and then also purchased a commercial building with my business partner. By 2019 time frame I started to see the effects of compounding as values going up and mortgage principle getting paid down by rents. It was then that I was able to see wealth creation at substantial levels. That sounds easier said than done, but it can put you on an easier path to financial freedom. Financial freedom means having control over your time. You're not relying on a third party or a job to tell you what to do and what not to do. Maybe you haven't even thought about the possibilities here. Maybe it seems unattainable to you right now. I'm here to tell you, it's possible. The little steps I'll teach you will compound over time, and you'll see the fruits of your labor.

Saving and investing has a passive bystander connotation and can often feel overwhelming. However, there are ways to strategize and actively turn the tables to win the game. Here at Strive, we look at saving and investing through the application of a competitive attack mindset. So if you are competitive, this is for you. If you don't consider yourself to be competitive, now is the time to learn!

Strive for 25 gets its name from the notion of helping people work toward increasing their savings and setting a goal to saving

25% of their income. This is a healthy goal to work toward because it is a proven path toward achieving financial freedom and independence.

Putting money into savings allows you the opportunity to acquire various types of assets and allows time and compounding interest to work for you. A perfect scenario is when your income from the assets purchased are high enough to sustain your lifestyle. This is described as being financially free - free to go do what you want because your lifestyle is sustained without having to work a job for someone else's business.

This e-book will provide an abundance of information and examples that will be helpful on your journey toward financial success. However, information is just one piece of the puzzle that we will talk more about in later chapters. If information were all we needed to be happy and successful, we would all be happy and successful! The internet is a one-stop-shop these days with virtually everything one would need in order to learn to be successful. However, most of us are aware that this is not the case.

In this e-book, we will outline some strategies and processes that will help you turn information into action in order to work toward your goals.

Upon completion, you will see ordinary things in a different light, and will know what it takes to make the slight changes that will shift your life into a direction full of abundance and prosperity.

Realistically, saving 25% of one's income may not be immediately achievable for everyone. But we will discuss why and how this process of striving toward this specific goal is vital for financial success, financial freedom, and financial independence.

The process towards this goal will change you as you learn new habits and make new connections that will help you along the way.

This book is about the how and why. Along the way we will identify some of the typical obstacles many of us hit that derail us from reaching our goals.

We will review the technical as well as the mental sides of the equation.

LeBron James is one of the best athletes the world has ever seen. He has won 4 NBA championships, all kinds of awards and had a streak of going to the NBA Finals 8 years in a row. 8 years! That is absolutely incredible. Going that deep into the NBA playoffs for that many years will certainly take its toll on the body and mind. But somehow, this man continues to show up every day for work and play at the highest level, and he makes it look easy.

And then came 2019. He had just moved to Los Angeles to join the Lakers. They had a thin roster and failed to make the playoffs.

This was unknown territory to a legend like LeBron James.

By this time, the school he helped open for the underprivileged in Akron, OH had just completed its first school year. With the absence of the NBA playoffs, he was able to give his body more time to recover and also spend more time at the school.

For someone who can dunk over seven footers, buy expensive houses in different parts of the country, get all the endorsements and be considered one of the greatest athletes of all time, the ability to invest your time and dollars in a project so impactful for kids who absolutely need it has to be so gratifying.

Isn't this what it is really all about? The fame, the fortune...when you drill down to the core of it, it's not about the tangible things. It's about the power of choice.

This is part of what draws us to celebrities and athletes and fame - we are drawn to the idea of being able to choose where and when we go on vacation, what businesses to open, what type of cars we drive, what type of charitable giving we can involve ourselves in.

There are so many entrepreneurs who have built this type of lifestyle that go under the radar of public fame but have built lives just like this. Maybe not to the same scale as LeBron James or Michael Jordan or Serena Williams, and obviously there are many people who want a similar lifestyle. But there are also many who don't want ALL OF THAT, but still want to get ahead, build a life of comfort, and stay ahead financially.

Our goal with this platform is to show the everyday person that there is a proven path to this type of life.

Why do we feel this is important?

Because it's not easy to do, and data reflects this. According to a recent Bankrate survey, over 50% of American adults don't have enough in savings to cover a 1,000 emergency!

But we know this is obtainable for you by implementing the strategies you are about to dive into.

Here at Strive for 25, we dig deep because the bottom line is, we believe the part we really want is the power to choose.

Drilling down on this notion of the Power to Choose is important because it allows us to provide more clarity of what financial success is.

You don't have to have the vocals and talent of Kelly Clarkson or Beyoncé to have financial freedom, or even be financially independent. You don't have to be a CEO of a publicly traded company.

There are so many examples of ordinary people who have used the resources and tools available to build an amazing life that includes this Extreme Power of Choice, regardless of the obstacles in front of them. We will share some examples later.

This is about showing every person that there is a path and a real possibility for you to make this a reality, whether or not you believe it right now.

As you continue, you will begin to see that this path is not as far out of reach or as complicated as you may think.

In fact, we will show the steps to get on that path toward financial success are actually pretty easy to do. It's not a cakewalk by any means, but the steps are attainable. And that is the difference between the best and the rest. These steps can be so easy that they seem insignificant, and those who are not truly committed will stop doing them.

Does building wealth and financial success and having this *Elite Power to Choose* sound like something that you want in your life?

Do you want to know what these step-by-step action items are?

If the answer is no, that is ok. We encourage you to read a little further to see if there is any spark of inspiration or info that can help you on your journey.

If the answer is yes, then buckle up! We are about to start a ride that will open up your eyes, your heart, and your mind to what is possible.

We will share some ideas and information that may be new to you. We'll also shed light on some things you already know, that will allow you to see these regular and ordinary things from a new perspective to produce more action and results.

Regardless of where you are on your journey, whether you are just starting or already well on your way toward financial freedom and financial independence, you will find value contained within these pages.

At the end of the day, it is all about leaving a legacy. Perhaps this content will help you specifically, or even better it may provide a space for you to share the wisdom you learn with others.

<u>What is Strive for 25?</u>

Strive for 25 literally means to build your way up to saving 25% of your income. If one is able to save 25% of their income, they will be well on their way to financial success, financial freedom, and potentially financial independence.

Obviously, this is a big goal. We know! On the surface, this could sound discouraging, or lead you to think it's not possible.

However, this is something we are very intentional about.

One thing we didn't ask above, is that just because it's possible, does that mean we can do it?

Even if we begin to believe that we can do it at some point in the future, then the question becomes….DO I WANT TO?

It seems really, really hard, so why do I want to endure all kinds of pain, stress and anxiety? For what? Why is it important to do so?

What if I do all that work and I never get to the point of saving 25% of my income? Then what? Will I obtain financial success or financial failure?

In the coming chapters we will address these questions.

We will map out why saving money is important, and share examples of ordinary people reaching unimaginable goals.

We will map out the "how." We will show the technical side of things, as well as a side that doesn't get talked about as much: understanding how the mind plays a part.

We will pull it all together and show you what it all means.

Next up, what is possible?

The Why: you put money away, buy assets, the assets build in value, and compound.

The How: Understand that regular, mundane tasks are important. It makes the difference between a life of abundance, versus a life of mediocrity.

Roadmap: how to apply the info.

We'll also cover:

- The things that stop most people
- Knowing the power of compounding
- Knowing the power of the subconscious
- Falling off
- Mapping out your why
- Action items to get there
- Remember that reaching your dreams means staying consistent!

Chapter Two: A Destination in Mind

In the last chapter we talked about "The Power of Choice," and we asked the question, "How does a regular person make this a reality?"

Before we can talk about how to get there, we have to know exactly where we are going. A popular scene in the film "Planes Trains and Automobiles" does a great job of teaching us all a lesson in truly knowing where we are going. (If you're not familiar with the Movie, ask your parents. Highly recommend it if you haven't seen it!)

In this scene, John Candy's character, Del Griffith, is driving down the highway late at night with Neal Page, played by Steve Martin. A car from across the way keeps honking their horn and yelling out the window at them over and over. Del finally notices them, looks over and thinks they are wanting to race, honks and yells back. Shortly after, Neal makes out what they are saying and tells Del, "They're saying we are going the wrong way."

Del replies, "Going the wrong way? Oh, must be drunk, how would he know where we're going?"

The scene concludes when they see two semis coming at them and realize they are going the wrong way down the highway - an impending crash ahead! They ultimately end up going right in between the two massive trucks, narrowly avoiding the crash and the calamity that would follow.

When we parallel this story to our lives, we challenge you to ask yourself these questions:

Do you know where you are headed on your own financial journey? Is it crystal clear, or is it murky?

Are you going the wrong way down a one lane road, with impending crashes ahead? As Candy says, "How do you know if you are going the right way if you don't know where you are going?"

At this moment in time, do you have any financial goals? And if you do, are they clear, specific and written down? Should we add a suggestion of where to write them down?

If the answer is yes, go ahead and write some of them down below. If the answer is no, that's ok. Our goal is to share some stories that will inspire you and some ideas to guide you with taking this first step.

In the next couple chapters, we are going to show you examples of regular people achieving massive amounts of wealth.

The goal is to show you what is possible.

That living a life of abundance and success is possible.

That a life with an extreme power of choice is possible.

Once we have built this foundation, we can then start talking about charting our own course.

Let's begin with George's story.

The Story of George

George is a recent graduate from a trade school and is now working as an apprentice making $15 per hour. He is a little bit of a partier and has a lot of friends he keeps up with. From a financial perspective, he's doing ok. He's not in a ton of debt. He earns decent pay but spends most of what he has, and his savings is not more than a couple hundred dollars.

One day he gets a phone call from a family member and receives news that he's going to get an inheritance of $50,000. He is so pumped! His first reaction is that he's going to quit his job and then…well, after the initial excitement wears off, he comes to his senses and realizes that he doesn't really know what he would do at that point if he were to quit his job.

The next week rolls around, and he shows up at work as usual. He goes on living the same way he was before, spending most of what he has coming in, but now he has 50k in the bank. Time goes on. Days pass, weeks pass, months pass.

That 50k in the bank is still sitting there. He didn't really know what to do with it. He didn't have anybody in his family or network that was extremely successful with money and didn't have anyone to rely on for financial advice.

He had heard stories of the stock market crash in 2008 and stories on the news about how the market now has increased so much and was ready for a major pull back. He was scared to put the money into anything.

A year went by, and then 2 years, and then 5 years. All the while, that 50k was still sitting in the bank.

That bank account was earning interest of .10%.

After 5 years that 50k had turned into a total of $50,250.50.

Yes that's right! Two hundred and fifty dollars and fifty cents.

Year 1: multiply 50k x .001 and you get $50.
Year 2: you take 50,050 x .001 and you get
$50.05.
Year 3: you take 50,100.05 x .001 and you get
50.10.
Year 4: you take 50,150.15 x .001 and you get
50.15.
Year 5: you take 50,200.30 x .001 and you get
50.20.

All together this adds up to 50,250.50.

Clearly this $250 return is not something that would get many excited, let alone put someone on the path of financial independence.

After the 5th year, he had finally become more aware of what he was missing out on with other opportunities to grow his investments. He decided to invest the money in the stock market.

In this example of the 50k invested in the S&P 500, how much do you think it would grow to over the long term? Over 5 years, 10 years, 20 Years, 30 years? 25 years, assuming a 10% return annually?

First, we are using 25 years because we are taking the 30 year chunk of time and then the first 5 years he had it stowed away in savings.

If we assume an average of 10% return, after 5 years, the account would grow to $80,525. In 20 years it would have grown to 336k. After 25 years, the account would have grown to 541k.

What if he would have started 5 years earlier? The 30 year total would have grown to 872k. (We are using 25 years because we are taking the 30 year chunk of time and then the first 5 years he had it stowed away in savings.)

The Story of Rebecca

Rebecca works with George at the same trade company. Even though they went to school together, they ran with different crowds and didn't really hang out.

At her first job, she was making about the same $15 per hour wage that George was making.

Rebecca had demonstrated a strong work ethic and had shown initiative to intentionally go out of her way to reach out to some of the veterans on the work teams to get extra tips and find ways to improve.

Along the way, her work had caught notice from Gabby, who was one of the team leaders. Not only was Gabby really good at her job and extremely knowledgeable, she was also financially savvy.

Gabby had received multiple raises over the years, had multiple rental properties and seemed to always be going on vacation in different parts of the country. She seemed to have everything figured out.

Rebecca obviously knew who Gabby was, but was caught by surprise when Gabby went out of her way to befriend her.

Gabby had seen that Rebecca was always one of the hardest working of the newcomer apprentices. Not only was she hard working, but Rebecca consistently showed that she was open to feedback and would implement the advice.

Along the way, Rebecca had asked Gabby if she would be willing to share some tips and insight on how she had been able to build up her finances so well and accumulate real estate.

Gabby was happy to share.

The first piece of advice she had was "keep things simple."

One way to keep things simple is to start with a **simple and achievable goal**.

The second piece of advice was to "Remove the thought" out of things. The more you have to think about down the road, the more it leaves the possibility of falling off track, getting distracted from the goal, or just flat out forgetting.

One way to do this is to **automate the process**. She gave 3 examples:

1) Automate your savings by setting up an **auto transfer**.

Example: if your monthly goal is $100 per month savings, setting up $50 auto transfers from checking into savings on each payroll day.

2) Aim to put away enough savings that can cover at least 3 months of expenses. This will be your Emergency Fund.

3) Buy assets. After you put enough savings away to set up your emergency funds, start to look at different assets: Stocks and index funds, Real Estate, Crypto Currency, NFTs, etc.

You buy assets like these with a long term goal. They will work for you day and night, increase in value and build wealth.

Rebecca took the advice to heart and that same night started making a plan. She set up an automatic transfer into her savings for the date of each pay period. She started with a goal of saving $100 per month, so she split that into $50 auto transfers twice a month on each pay date.

This had been working successfully, and she wasn't even noticing the missing $100 each month.

This strategy allowed her to put money away immediately and had the psychological effect of cultivating the discipline to live off of what was left. By taking thought out of the equation, it removed the possibility of distraction, forgetting and any other obstacles that could prevent her from logistically putting $100 into her savings account each month.

She then researched more about the best way to start investing in the stock market. She read up on mutual funds, individual stocks and bonds, index funds and ETFs, and financial advising companies.

She got a little overwhelmed and went back to Gabby for advice.

Gabby couldn't tell her what to do with her money or give financial advice. However, she explained that while there are some good options out there, her best course of action would be to start with Index funds and continue to educate herself.

From her research, she knew that the **S&P 500 ETF Index** is considered one of the benchmark Index Funds. This Exchange Traded Fund (ETF) has the ticker symbol SPY on the New York Stock Exchange, and tracks the biggest 500 companies in the United States. One of the benefits is that its expense ratio is very low, at about .10%.

Note: Expense ratio is something that is part of every index fund or mutual fund. It is the fee or cost for the fund to manage the fund.

Should we give an example of how many months it took her to build her emergency fund?

She started with her first $100 and put this into the SPY index fund. She also set this up on an auto transfer so that the $100 went directly into an online brokerage and automatically purchased shares or fractional shares from each payroll check.

The first example of compounding we used before was just taking a lump sum of 50k, with a defined interest rate of 0.10% and applying over a period of time. This example was using a simple interest calculation.

Rebecca's example is a little bit more complicated. Instead of a lump sum that just sits and compounds over time, we are going to be adding additional funds each month. Also, the rate of return in the stock market is going to be much different than a very simple and safe bank savings account. Bank interest is low risk and inherently has a very low interest rate.

The reason it is low risk is because the deposits in a bank that are FDIC insured are guaranteed up to 250k by the federal government. Because of that guarantee, the money is safe. Risk and reward: low risk means low reward so the return of interest on money tends to be low compared to other asset classes.

However, with inflation increasing so rapidly in the last 12 months or so, we have seen interest rates go up, and the bank interest on savings accounts also go up.

Whereas, in the stock market the rate of return can be much higher. Over 100 years the average return is about 10% before taxes. However, there is a risk when investing in the stock market. Over a long period of time the returns are substantial, but in shorter time frames, there are periods where stocks go down, and some drop drastically.

The most recent example is the crash of 2008, where the stock market plummeted over 50% over a period of months. However, since recovering from the lows, the S&P 500 has risen about 200% from its pre-crash highs from 2007.

Before the crash, the S&P 500 Index was around the 150 level in late 2007. By March of 2009 it had dipped to 67, about 55% drop. As of October 2021, it was hit 450, which was three times what it was in 2007. And Shortly after the Index hit 488 in November 2021. There after into 2022, the Index bottomed at about 350, and has since been hovering between 420 and 380. (As of April 2023)

100% return would mean going from 150 to 300. 200% return would mean going from 150 to 450

In Rebecca's example of investing $100 each month at 10% rate of return, what will that come out to be?

After the first year she would have put away $1,200, and the total would be about $1,256 - in other words, earning about $56 of appreciation in the first year.

Over the first 5 years, she would have put away $6,000 and it would have turned into $7,745. Meaning $1,745 in appreciation.

Who would you rather be? George with the 50k earnings and earning .10% interest in a savings account? Or Rebecca who is saving $100 per month and earning 10% with a little over 7k put away after 5 years?

After 10 years have passed, she would have put in $12,000 and that would have turned into a little over 20k.

After 20 years, she would have put in 24k that will turn into about 75k.

After 30 years, she will have put in 36k and that will turn into 226k.

Now who would you rather be?

Would you rather be George? If he had stuck on his original path of the first 5 years earning 0.10%, he would have a total of $51,150 after 30 years.

Or would you rather be Rebecca? She started putting away $100 each month and stuck to her plan over 30 years, and she turned 36k into 226k - multiplying her money 6 times over.

This is an example of the power of compounding. Can you see how compounding can have an exponential effect on your money?

Is 226k a number that gets you excited? Is 226k something you can see yourself retiring on in 30 years and being able to do all the things that you want to do?

Maybe yes, but perhaps you're thinking, "No way."

But wait, I thought we were talking about opportunity and possibility, and the extreme power of choice.

226k would be an amazing success, but that number does not get me excited when we are talking 30 years from now. And when you throw in inflation that is a whole different story.

Well, how do we get to a scenario or number that can gets you jumping for joy?

In the next chapter we will add another component to this story, and we will see what you think.

Compounding Applied to Another Element

In that last scenario we were saving $100/month and investing in the S&P ETF with an assumed 10% rate of return. In doing so, Rebecca turned 36k into 226k.

Rebecca had been inspired by Gabby and what she was able to accomplish in a short period of time:

- Started with her company at an apprentice level making $15 an hour.

- She shared rent with two other friends

Just like George, things were tight and she was just getting by. However, she had set out a defined target for saving money each month, put it on autopilot, moved forward with the plan, and stayed focused.

That sounds simple and easy. But wait!

In the real world, life is not just a math formula. Life is not linear.

We have good days and bad days.

Things come up that we may not expect, like a flat tire, or a fluke illness, medical bills, etc.

But it's more than that.

When we are in our late teens and early twenties, our circle of friends is typically bigger than when we get into our 30's or

40's and beyond. What does that mean for our budget and expenses?

Your friends invite you to go out and meet up two nights a week.

But it's more than that!

It's the three 21st birthday parties in a 6 week span. It's the wedding showers and wedding gifts. Your college friends come to town and you have to find time to meet up with them for dinner and drinks.

It's the deposit for an apartment, furnishing your apartment, it's the down payment for a car. This stuff adds up over the course of a year.

However, for Rebecca, after all the ups and downs, the two steps forward and 3 steps back and then 3 steps forward and then 2 steps back, she was able to put away $100 on average each month.

Again, life is not always linear, and we can't expect it to be. When the car needed an oil change and tire rotation, Rebecca had to dip into some of her savings to help cover. But she was determined to stay on course with her plan. She knew she needed to figure out a way to make up the extra savings.

Maybe it's a combination of picking up extra shifts and getting overtime, as well as consciously skipping a couple weekends of happy hours that she otherwise would have gone to.

Again, not a scientific formula. But through sheer determination, dedication, and creativity she found a way to make it happen and get to the annual goal of $1,200.

Some of Rebecca's friends questioned why she wasn't able to come out as much anymore. But for Rebecca, she knew there was an opportunity in front of her. And if she didn't stay on course, she would lose the opportunity to achieve her dreams. She knew if she was not moving forward, she was moving backward.

There is no in between.

She truly understood how important the power of compounding is and she wanted to use it for her benefit, not against her.

Then came year 2.

Rebecca had picked up some extra shifts and started working alongside Roger. Roger was one of the top specialists in his field and Rebecca had picked up some tips and efficiencies just by watching. She decided to proactively ask Roger if he would spend some time with her to share more insight, tips and advice on the job.

Roger happily agreed. From their conversations, there was one major point that Roger talked about that really stood out and left an impression on her.

He talked about how he was constantly searching for a way to get better every day. It didn't matter how much better, but just something each day. He explained that his goal was to "find my fraction of a fraction every day."

Roger explained further that his goal was to build on that gain every day. Because if you can get better 1% every day, that percentage adds up over time. 1% every day for 365 days is obviously well over 300 percent.

Who wouldn't want to apply that kind of improvement to a goal?

Even a fraction of a percent each day can be substantial when you compound it every day over the course of a year, or years. For example, 0.1% every day is over 36% improvement over the course of 365 days. Hence his "fraction of a fraction" mantra.

Rebecca appreciated that conversation and advice. She even started trying to consciously think each day about finding that fraction of a fraction. Over the course of the next few weeks she realized that she was doing it some days and other days she would simply forget, or not know what to look for.

So she went back to Roger and asked for more advice on how he was so good at finding his fraction of a fraction.

Roger explained that when he first started going down this path, he was inconsistent with it as well. But he tried something that ended up working for him.

He started to write down that one thing every day. A week went by, a month went by, 2 months went by and he did it every single day without fail. He'd reached a point where he wanted it so bad that he couldn't not do it.

This process of writing that one thing down each day had become a habit. This habit became so strong that if a day went by and he was lying in bed and hadn't done it, the alarm bells would go off in his head to get it done.

That's when the light bulb went on for Rebecca. Now she understood!

Roger's concept of finding a fraction of a fraction to get better each day was taking the force of compounding and applying it to something other than money. This was compounding being applied toward perfecting his craft.

Then with him building the habit of writing down that one thing every day, this was applying the same force of compounding to the building of the habit: building a habit of building the habit.

Rebecca went to work. She continued working at her craft on the job. Got a raise. Made more money.

She got better at her budget, and saved more money.

Year 2 she updated her plan to save $200 per month, meaning $100 per pay period.

She continued on her path, continued to climb the ranks at her job, got pay raises and continued to work the plan. And in year 3 she upped her savings to $300 per month.

In year 4, she was able to continue on the same path and up the savings to $400 per month.

She continued this trend each year, increasing the amount by $100.

By year 10, saving $1,200 per month, year 20, saving $2,400 per month, etc.

When you map out the numbers of a period of 30 years what would you guess that the total would come out to be?

Over that time span we would have put in about 560k into our stock investments, and after 30 years we would have a little over **2 million dollars.**

We started at $100 per month, and $1200 put away after the first year. But with the right focus and using the force of compounding to her advantage, plus perfecting her craft, she was able to build a substantial amount of wealth.

So let me ask you, is **2 million dollars** something you would get excited about? Even after 30 years?

For many I think the answer would be an astounding yes. For others, maybe…maybe not.

For those who aren't excited, that's ok. This illustration shows the power of compounding on dollars, but then also applying to other things like improving your craft.

Right now, we are just talking about fine tuning a vision of what gets you excited, and some of the core principles. Later we will dig into more about vision and the how.

In the next chapter, we will talk about another way to accumulate assets and build wealth.

The Story of Gentry

Real Estate Compounding

There was a fourth friend who was connected to Gabby and Rebecca. His name is Gentry, and he was actually a third cousin of Gabby. He had stayed in touch with Gabby and Roger all the way through high school.

Gentry finished college, and was just beginning his career in the analytics field. He was renting a house with a couple of college friends and trying to squeeze out some savings each month to try and get ahead.

He met a unique individual one morning at a coffee shop. This person is someone he had seen before because he was a regular. Gentry would always go in, get his drink and leave in the mornings. When he would stop in it was always at the same time, around 7:15am, which gave him time to get to work on time. And every time he would see Jeff at a table in the back reading. He bumped into Jeff one day while in line, and initiated a conversation. Gentry mentioned he had seen him multiple times before, reading either a paperback or on his phone.

Today he was on his phone, and Gentry asked Jeff what he was reading. He explained that it was a book called "Rich Dad, Poor Dad." He told Gentry that if you ever want to build assets for yourself and get out of the rat race, then this book was a must read.

Some of the key insights include:

- Poor and middle class work for money. The rich have money work for them.

- Rich people acquire assets, the poor and middle class acquire liabilities.

I absolutely recommend this book, as it is an important foundational tool to start building the right mindset for building wealth.

Jeff also explained that another book he had been reading was on computer coding. He had picked up a side hustle, and it was something that was allowing him to earn some extra money on the side. The cool thing was that it had also made him more valuable at his current job, and he received a couple raises way faster than other people in his department.

This single conversation with Jeff was a turning point in Gentry's life. The light bulb was going off!! He was beginning to see an opportunity to get ahead and start to build a pathway for not having to rely on regular job for the long term. He started to realize he could acquire assets, and some day down the road have income from the assets replace the income from his job. In the books he was reading, this was called Financial Freedom.

He continued learning and researching, and decided that he wanted to begin accumulating real estate.

He talked to a mortgage lender about purchasing a home. Unfortunately, he was soon disappointed to find out his credit scores were in the 550's, didn't have any savings, and didn't qualify.

He didn't know what to do next, he had this burning desire to build a real estate portfolio. But was so shook, he put it on the back burner.

A few months later, ran into Jeff again at the coffee shop. In the conversation, Gentry mentioned the update about the real estate plan:

"Yeah my credit score was 550, no savings, and told me I didn't qualify...."

"Ok, well you're 21, so that's not surprising. How many accounts do you have reporting on your profile?"

"Just one... a credit card... and some student loans, oh and my car loan I got about 10 months ago"

"So did they give you a plan?"

"No"

"Wait, then didn't tell you what to work on to get your scores up?

"No"

"Holy Expletive... (paused for a few seconds)

So you just stopped??   If you want something bad enough, which I know you do, you can't just let one set back stop you from reaching your goal.

The best, the greats, they don't stop. They see a goal and vision, and they don't stop till that goal becomes a reality. Literally every day, they take one step towards that vision.

Ok. This is what you're going to do.

You're going to call my person Rachel. Talk to her, and do everything she tells you to do. And then call me after you talk to her.

So Gentry reached out to Rachel. They worked on a plan to tweak a few things, and helped boost the credit scores.

The other thing they discussed was his lack of savings.

They reviewed is overall situation in terms of income and expenses. At that time, he had rent, a car payment, gas, groceries, car insurance, etc... the basic expenses and there was nothing left over. There was nothing he could cut.

Rachel explained, "Ok, have you ever heard of the Savings Equation?"

"No...but like just about how to save money?

"Yeah, exactly. If I asked you what the equation is, can you take a guess?

"Ok, so you work a job, you make money and then you have expenses, and if you have money left over that is your savings."

"Exactly!"

Simply: Income - Expenses = Savings

This is the first part of the Wealth Equations.

There are three and they are very simple, but powerful.

Savings equation..... wait, and pulls out a piece of paper from her bag. Here is an illustration. This is something that we teach.

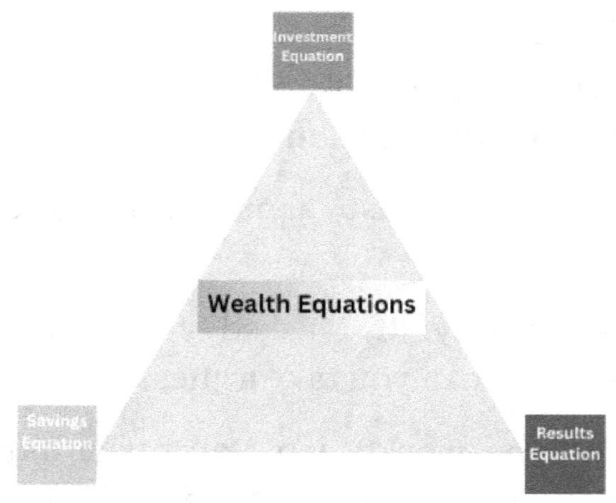

The three equations are Savings Equation, Investment Equation, and the Results Equation.

The savings equation is simple, as we just discussed. The investment equation is also simple. You buy an asset, get a rate return, and over a period of time, and that is your total return.

Asset x ((Expected Rate of Return) ^ Time) = Total Return

The Third Equation is the Results Equation.

She explained, this is something that is not as concrete as a math equation. However, we have defined it as this:

So many people know what they want to do, but just don't do it. Whether it be get a better job, be in a better relationship, save money, invest, better health or in better shape, the list goes on.   They know what they want, but so many just don't do it. and they remain stuck, in their comfort zone.

The stuff that you think about all day, literally becomes your results. We operate off of subconscious programs all day. Stuff we don't even consciously think about.

Your thoughts, affects you how you feel, which affects your actions, which over time becomes your results.

Thoughts=> Emotions=> Actions = Results

Right now, you are in a position that you have nothing to cut out of your budget.

There is so much content out there about doing budgets, cutting expenses and not enough about the other part of the equation, which is what?

"Income"

Yes!!! So what are you going to do?

"Increase income?"

"Yes, that is an option"

So what are you going to do?

"Go get a second job.....as we have been talking I remembered that a friend of mine's dad was looking for some help on the weekends for their business. And it's actually something that is in a similar field of what I'm already doing, just like you mentioned.

So within about 2 months, Gentry started earning an extra 1k per month. For him the paycheck took about 30% out for taxes and social security, etc. so the net was about $700 per month.

He had then set up his lifestyle to live off his main job's income, and the second job money went straight into a bank account that he didn't touch.

Instantly he was saving about 20% of his total gross income.

So he was back on track for his vision of building a real estate portfolio.

His goal was to find a modest home as a stepping stone to be able to live there for a couple of years, and then purchase the next home and turn the old one into a rental. He had been targeting a home in the 150k range, and found one with 2 bedrooms and 1 bath.

Gentry had saved enough money for the 3.5% down payment for an FHA Loan ($5,250), plus enough for the closing costs. Once he closed on the home, he was excited to have a home he could call his own. And instead of paying someone else's mortgage, he was in a position to start building equity for himself.

He continued to read, learn, and connect with people who he could learn from about building wealth. He was determined to continue saving money so that he could be prepared to purchase the next home.

He stayed in touch with Rachel and they continued to talk about Gentry's plan for building a real estate portfolio.

Rachel explained that, "yeah, your plan of buying the next one as a primary residence and turn the old one into a rental, we call that the "Stair Step Method. As someone continues to stack properties.

There is an example that we share often, that illustrates the power of real estate.

Would like me to share it?

"Well of course. "

Let's say you have 10,000 and put it in the stock market for a year, and get a very good return of 10%. How much return would you have in that year?

"Well. That would be 1,000"

Yep! Ok, now let's say another option would be to take that same 10,000 and use it as a down payment to purchase a 300k home. and let's say that the home appreciates 3% in the first year, how much would the return be?

"Ok, well that would be 'Nine hund....' Wait no… that would be 'Nine Thousand' "

"YES!!!!! You got it!!"

Holy expletive that's a 9 to 1 difference, 9k vs 1k.

And imagine that difference over 10 years, 20 years, 30 years, especially if you start to stack real estate purchases.

Ok, I get it!!!

"So coming in to year 3, he continued to save and was ready to purchase the 2nd home. This time, his scores continued to build and he was in the 700's.

He had identified a home at 250k.   This home was a little bit bigger - 3 bedrooms, 2 bathrooms and more square footage. Because he needed more space and the house was an upgrade, the lender was able to call it a primary residence and allow for the 5% down payment ($12,500). .

(Note: Typical investment property purchases require more money down, such as 15% to 25% down payment.)

He had been planning this and had renters already lined up. They were friends of his, and he was able to set up a lease amount that was $300 more than the mortgage payment. The cash flow was minimal after some expenses, but he was in a position where his tenants were paying his mortgage and helping him build equity. He had acquired an asset that was working for him, and had taken the next step on his journey to building wealth.

Values continued to rise about 3% year after year. The renter continued to pay down the mortgage balance and his equity (ownership in the home) was still building.

Gentry got a new job with a pay increase and was able to set aside more money. Things were going well for him! He was on a mission to continue acquiring assets and build wealth. He was now in a place in life where he was engaged and getting married soon, and it was going to be time to purchase another home.

By that time, it had been 4 years since he had purchased the first home and 2 years from buying the 2nd. The first home had increased in value 3% each year and gone from $150,000 up to $168,000. The mortgage was paid down from $142,500 to $131,000. So far, he had accumulated $37,000 in equity.

The second home purchase for $250,000 had increased in value from $250,000 to $265,000 and the mortgage balance was paid down from $237,500 to $228,000. There was now $37,000 in equity in only two years. In just 4 years, Gentry had paid $20,000 in down payments and the equity built to roughly $63,000.

It's true that the markets don't always go up in a straight line, but we are assuming they will increase by 3% each year. However, short term fluctuations can cause prices to either decrease or increase more than this amount for a period of time before reverting back down again.

As the 4th year on the journey was coming to a close, his confidence and belief in his skills were growing. He continued to put money away. This was due to a combination of getting better at his job, managing expenses, and also creating a side job doing work on Fiverr.com to make extra money.

As the year turned, he was already targeting the next home. In a short period of time, a lot had changed in his personal life. He'd gotten married a year prior, and they just found out they had a baby on the way. Their goal was to purchase a home with a little extra space, and again turn the old one into a rental.

So in year 5, they ended up purchasing a home for 350k, and were again able to get a low down payment mortgage with 5% down ($17,500) because the next purchase was an upgrade with their change in needs.

Unlike last time where Gentry had time to source a renter through his network, he didn't have the capacity to do that again. Instead, he was able to utilize his real estate agent to list the rental and find a renter.

He continued down this path. Their family continued to grow, and it again became time for more space.

At the beginning of year seven he purchased his fourth property for $450,000. He put down his normal 5% which was $22,500. His realtor again was able to find a renter for the departure residence.

At this point, things had settled and they were going to be staying put for a while.

Fast forwarding to the end of year ten….Gentry had purchased four properties and put in $60,000 of down payment money. The total value of real estate had risen to $1.446 Million. The total mortgage balances had been paid down to a total of about 999k. At that point the equity had built up to about $447,000.

At that point in time, Gentry was 33 years old, and had been on this path for over 10 years now.

He had friends, colleagues, and acquaintances that he knew with similar age and background who were still renting. While owning real estate is not for everyone and comes with inherent risks, it seemed that many were missing out on an opportunity to build wealth.

He was able to capitalize on some of the tools available, build wealth and turn $60k into 368k after 10 years. Again, he had to pay a mortgage payment each month, but the alternative is paying rent, as a housing expense is a basic necessity.

Chapter Three: Risks and Rewards

The risks of owning real estate and being a landlord are real.

We won't be going into high detail here about it, as the core message is about the opportunity.

 Gentry was able to account for these assumed risks by having good homeowners insurance, hiring a management company, and also building up additional emergency savings earmarked for real estate portfolio expenses, and the 'what-ifs.'

Gentry, similar to Gabby, had been utilizing the force of compounding on real estate.

How much equity would have been built if you fast forward the clock 20 years?

The value of the properties would have increased to $1.951 million and the mortgage balances paid down to 682k. The equity built up would project to $1.269 million. Again: $60,000 into $1.269 million in 20 years.

What about 30 years?

Care to guess???

The value of the properties would have increased to $2.633 Million and the mortgage balances paid down to 216k. The equity built up would project to $2.417 million.

Is that a number that gets you excited?

Some may say yes, some may say no, but the data that is out there shows that the average net worth of a person in their 50s could range from 833k to 1.175 million.

The average also can be considered a skewed calculation due to the top 1% having amassed such massive wealth that the numbers are not representative of a true average of the majority.

Another metric is the median. This calculation pulls the number from the direct middle of the group; meaning if there are 100 people in the room, the median pulls the wealth from the middle or 50th person on the ranking.

Here are some additional illustrations on the top 1% in net worth.

https://www.forbes.com/sites/tommybeer/2020/10/08/top-1-of-us-households-hold-15-times-more-wealth-than-bottom-50-combined/?sh=1c96a3235179

According to the latest Fed data, the top 1% of Americans have a combined net worth of $34.2 trillion (or 30.4% of all household wealth in the U.S.), while the bottom 50% of the population holds just $2.1 trillion combined (or 1.9% of all wealth).

The Fed estimates that the wealthiest 10% of Americans hold more than 88% of all available equity in corporations and mutual fund shares (with just the top 1% controlling more than twice as much equity as the bottom 50% of all Americans combined).

https://www.nerdwallet.com/article/finance/average-net-worth-by-age

Average net worth by age

Net worth totals vary by education, age, income and other factors. We'll focus on the median and average net worth figures for different age groups:

Age of head of family	Median net worth	Average net worth
Less than 35	$13,900	$76,300
35-44	$91,300	$436,200
45-54	$168,600	$833,200
55-64	$212,500	$1,175,900
65-74	$266,400	$1,217,700
75+	$254,800	$977,600

The typical mortgage is 30 years, and the first home mortgage would be paid in full, and then the rest of the homes would have balances remaining according to the remaining term. For example, the last home would have about 6 years remaining.

So a Net Worth over 2 million dollars in our fifties or sixties is going to well exceed the median net worth in the mid 200's.

Can you begin to see how this all fits together, and rewarding it can be to allow for your power of compounding to work for you instead of against you?

Additionally, we used a conservative estimate on home appreciation of 3% for the projections.   Historically it's been around 4%. So if we apply 4% for the home appreciation instead of the 3% that would mean the real estate portfolio would be over 3 million instead of 2+ million.

Though this is a brief overview, there's more to it than what you just read. We didn't talk about closing costs for each property; that would be additional money needed and the risks of renters damaging said properties, which can cost an owner plenty in repairs or even replacement if they're not careful enough with their tenant selection process! And then we have management fees which vary depending on where your rental units are located.

Again, this is to illustrate the power of compounding. There are a number of ways to build wealth. Some people think they need to have a billboard top song, or throw a 98 mph fastball in order build substantial wealth but that's **simply not true**. The power behind compounding can help you build your own fortune.

<u>Then what?</u>

Gabby's 2 million dollar stock portfolio shows the compound effect on money and investing in the stock market. (See appendix note where we take that 560k invested, and applied to real estate)

Gentry's story showed the compound effect when applied to real estate, and turned 60k into over 2 million.

Is a $2 million portfolio of stocks or real estate, or both, something that motivates you to want to put in the work?

I think many will say yes to this question. But now what?

What happens next?

Is this the inspiration you need to go out there and get on the path to make this a reality?

This is where the wrench gets thrown.

What we know is excitement isn't the end game - getting it done is.

In the pages that follow, we will share tried and true principles around helping solidify your beliefs that you can reach amazing heights. This is something that we expand on and take even further with the folks who choose to join us on their own strive for 25 journeys.

Chapter Four: Stay the Path, Reach Your Goals

Just like people who make New Year's Resolutions, most start off on track after a few days, or the first week. But then some fall off the wagon. What about after 2 weeks? Even more have fallen off the wagon and stopped working toward their goal. What about 1 month? 2 months?

By this time, the majority have fallen off their path.

Why?

Maybe you just forgot over time? Maybe the goal just wasn't really that important to you, so you stopped. Or maybe you started out excited for a week, 2 weeks, but didn't see the results, so you stopped. Many can relate to this!

But what if that person keeps working towards their goal after a month, 2 months, 6 months, a year? The results will become tangible, visible and undeniable!

The crazy thing is that the results in the first days, weeks, and months are there. They are just so tiny - fractions of a fraction of a percent - that they are not visible to the naked eye.

But when you allow time to work to your benefit, the power of compounding has the room it needs to create massive results for you!

Have you been to a motivational speech? Or watched a motivational movie scene? Or a motivational video on YouTube like a Ted talk? In that moment, how motivated are you? Are you supercharged to go tackle some goal, and make things happen? Energized? Pumped up?

So what happens in an hour? In 2 hours? Does that excitement wear off just a little bit?

What about after a day? For most, that excitement probably wears off just a little bit more.

What about after a week, and then a month?

That excitement and energy may have faded away altogether.

Something that could have been so amazing, and had a massive impact for yourself and those around you, faded into the wind.

How many times has this happened to you?

How much is this costing you? In dollars?, Better health? Better relationships? What about overall wellbeing?

When the next opportunity shows up in front of you and you have the ability to seize it, do you move forward or let it pass you by? If opportunities pass you by and you don't find a way to have the traction to seize the opportunity, isn't it easy to lose confidence in your abilities to improve your situation?

This is one of the most important parts of what we want to show you - that right here, right now, you have the opportunity to capitalize on the opportunity that is in front of you.

It will be different for every person.

If you can uncover the belief in yourself this can elevate you to a higher level!

Going back to the inspirational speech - let's say you have two people who attended that same speech.

One person in that moment writes down a couple notes about what they want to accomplish and several tangible action items that it would take to work towards that goal. After the speech they make a plan to review their chosen plan every single day.

The second person does not do this.

When we roll the clock forward, and the first person looks at their notes every single day over the course of weeks, and months, and years, and compare that to the second person who doesn't, who do you think has a greater chance of reaching their goal?

Common sense says that the person who builds a habit of reviewing their goal and action plan every day would have a better chance than the person who doesn't.

Easy to do, but also easy not to do. And that becomes the difference between the best and the rest.

This brings us to the second force that is crucial to understand if you want to increase your chances of reaching your goals.

That is the power of the subconscious mind.

The conscious mind is the part of the mind that pertains to active thinking, sensations, feelings, memories and emotions.

When you are consciously thinking about a math problem, having a conversation with someone over the phone, or thinking about which route to take when there is an accident, these are all part of our conscious mind that are actively working on a task.

It is a powerful tool and can be laser-focused on the task at hand of processing information and solving problems.

It does have a limitation though. For the conscious mind to work at its best, it typically needs to focus on one thing at a time.

While the conscious mind is at its best focused on one thing at a time, the subconscious mind has the ability to pick up where the conscious mind has left off. The subconscious mind is built to multi-task.

The subconscious mind is the part of our mind that performs tasks or actions that we don't actively think about.

A good example is the person who is driving home from work after a long day, and multi-tasking. Driving during rush hour traffic, running late for dinner, needing to stop at the store to pick up a couple ingredients, and simultaneously on the phone, making turns and getting off at exits, and at the end arrives home safely without consciously thinking about it.

How does this happen?

If it is the first time driving somewhere, or even within the first few times, it wouldn't be possible to get to the destination without looking at directions. But after multiple times, the directions have been programmed into a part of your mind that allows you to perform the process or action without it being at the forefront of your mind.

This is the brains way of conserving energy, and allowing to use energy toward other new things.

What if you could harness this same type of power to help you reach another type of destination, such as a goal in business or your personal life?

What if you could harness the power of the subconscious mind to help you reach your financial AND non-financial goals?

Imagine what could be possible then?

We have been talking about financial success, building wealth, and creating a life of abundance and extreme choice. And we have talked about the things that stop us from reaching our goals, such as distractions and not following through, and negative self-talk. Telling yourself you can't do it, the doubts that creep into our mind.

We discussed an example of writing down your 'why' and several action items, and then reviewing it every day.

This is a perfect example of programming directions into your subconscious mind.

We are using the conscious mind intentionally to link these directions to our subconscious mind.

Memory works in different ways. Are there certain things in your younger years that stand out and you remember?

Maybe it was a graduation day, or a certain party, or a certain game or match, or a very important conversation.

Take any of these examples, and what do you remember about the events that led up to it or the events thereafter? A lot of it goes unnoticed in our memories. Why?

Because these major things we remember trigger very strong emotions, whether they are happy, sad, proud, angry, disappointed, etc. These memories are anchored by very strong emotions, and is why we can access them readily in our minds.

There is another way to program the subconscious mind and that is through repetition. Have you heard of muscle memory?

Maybe it's playing the piano, or playing a sport, or even making a sandwich.

When you are making a peanut butter and jelly sandwich, are you thinking about opening the bread, the peanut butter and the jelly and thinking about the spread of each?

Probably not. This process has been programmed in our subconscious mind, and into muscle memory.

This may sound easy, but it takes work!

Building a habit is one of the hardest things to do. If I said hey, "if you can push a button at 12 clock for the next 30 days consecutively, you will win one million dollars"…could you do it?

I bet many could do that. However, some may not be able to stay on track for 30 straight days.

Now what if I said to push that button for 30 straight days, and then 30 more, and then 30 more, for a full year, and you would be on the road to building millions in wealth? Could you do that?

Some yes, some no. If you are in a place where you are standing still, just hovering above water, and don't feel like you are heading the right direction financially, this is what it will take.

This is what it will take to transform your life, to transform the way you think, the way you feel, your relationships, your health.

Programming the direction that you want in life is one powerful way to jump start your path to a life of abundance, richness and wealth. When you can prove to yourself that you can build a habit and do something 30 days in a row, you will know that you can literally do anything.

This doesn't have to be financial. It can be applied to health, wellness, and relationships.

When you get to that point, you will have unlocked one of the secrets that the best of the best already know. You will have unlocked a superpower.

In this eBook, we are focusing on finances and we will continue down this path as we round the remaining pages. But just know that this can be applied to any goal you desire.

Let's bring it all together.

What do you want?

What do you want your life to look like? What are your goals and aspirations financially?

Do you want to own a business? What will your business accomplish, and be known for? How much money will you need to get started and stay on track?

Do you want to own a real estate portfolio? How many properties do you want? Where will they be?

The more specific you can get, the more the emotions will allow you to anchor this into your subconscious as you program it over the days to come.

Now take some time to DREAM.

What do you want this to look like? Where do you want to be?

What are the steps to get there? Some may say work backward. That's up to you.

What do you need to do over the next 12 months?

Let's say you want to start a business. You'll need 50k to start the business and you want to start it in 6 months.

You identify that there is a way to save 2k per month by adjusting several things in your life. This could be a combination of cutting expenses, and adding in a second job to earn extra income.

Why: Because I am going to be the proud owner of a ____ business.

I will have 50k to start the business by July of this year.

I will work 12 extra hours a week to earn extra income

I will plan 5 days of meals in advance to stay within budget.

I will read 5 minutes every day of a self-development or business-oriented book.

This is POSSIBLE and would be an amazing start on your journey.

So take some time to map out your own 'why' and actions items.

We will do another exercise mirroring Rebecca.

I want to build a life of wealth and prosperity and have a net worth of 1 million dollars by the time I'm 40 so I can be financially independent in order to have the time to do xyz (run seminars, teach, help those in economic need, etc.)

Put it into Action!

Action item #1
Put $100 into savings each pay period.

Action item #2
Find one thing each week that can help me improve at my job, and write it down.

Action item #3
Read 5 minutes of a good book; Rich Dad Poor Dad: 7 Habits of Highly Effective People is a great option.

Action item #4
Is to the power of compounding. This is important because it helps to realign our expectations. In this society we are programmed to expect things to happen right now, whether it be the internet, on our phones, door dash food, etc.

Farmers get it. They understand the 9 month cycle and harvest because it is their livelihood. If information was all we needed to be happy and successful, we would all be happy and successful. But that is not the case, as over half of Americans don't have more than $400 in savings.

It takes more than that.

If you have a supercomputer but don't have the software installed to run the programs, it may be difficult to solve a problem.

All the information you need is out there, but you need the right equipment and understand how to use it in order to apply it to your benefit.

Using some of the principles outlined in this book could be part of the solution - the key to unlocking the next door to reaching your unlimited potential.

This book is about getting to the next level, wherever that may be for you.

Because once you get going, the next chapter of your life will be about obtaining the next level of success.

With these examples that show different ways individuals are choosing to shape their lives and investment futures, we have an opportunity to anchor some important points into several categories.

Everything we have discussed can be broken down into three categories, and each of these categories is an equation.

Here are the 3 equations:

Investment equation:

Purchase asset x (get a rate of return ^ Time)

Savings Equation:

Income minus expenses = savings

Results Equation:

Thoughts => feelings => Actions = Results

VISION and QUESTIONS you must answer for yourself:

What amount of money would I like to make?
What places do I want to visit?
What type of job would I like to have one day?
What do I want to give back to the world?
What do I want to be known for?

Create a Vision Board. When we have a crystal clear vision for our life, there is a strong connection between the sacrifices we must take today to have our vision become a reality in the future.

Who do I want to be professionally and personally?

What do I want to do professionally and personally?

What things do I want to have professionally and personally?

Answer the questions here:

Chapter Five: Courageous Goal Setting

Dream; unplug

Before we explain more about the 25%, there is a story we want to highlight. The 4 minute mile record was broken by Robert Banister in 1954, but before that it had been a milestone that was just out of reach for the best of the best runners for centuries. Experts believed that the 4 minute mile was not humanly possible.

There are even stories of runners tying bulls behind them to increase drive to do the impossible of cracking 4 minutes.

But when Roger Banister broke the 4 minute barrier at 3 minutes 59.40 seconds in 1954, it opened up the door to the impossible for so many more.

John Landy surpassed that level and ran a mile in 3 minutes and 58 seconds just a few months later in early 1955.

By 1962, four college athletes had run sub 4 minute miles and today, there are over 1400 athletes who have cracked 4 minutes.

Once that record was cracked, it became obtainable and the flood gates opened with more people believing they could obtain it, and they did.

What can we learn from this?

Saving 25% of your income may not be presently obtainable by the level of your income and current expenses. And you may not have any idea of how to get there at this moment in time. That is ok!

But I assure you that there are many people out there who are executing this feat. I am proof of that, because I personally am one of them.

It took me years to get here. And there many other people in our community that are there, and many more that are marching down that path.

Knowing that is possible is one important step in the process, as the 4 minute mile illustrates.

As Gentry worked with Rachel reassess his finances, the work they did together also expanded his way of thinking. This helped him see that there was another way to start saving money, and also strengthen his why (build portfolio of real estate to help get out of the rat race),

Wherever you fall on this range is ok. This is your time to dream. This is your time to think about and visualize the things that you are passionate about, and the things that inspire you.

So take a few moments to imagine what you would really like to do.

For example, imagine:

- You can spend your vacation doing what you want

- You can enjoy several weeks at one of the beach properties that you own and rent out most of the year through a management company

- You can donate whatever you want to the charity you feel most passionate about

- You can own a business

- You can start a charity foundation

Write down some of the things you would like to do if you had the money to do what you want.

Chapter Six: Strive for 25

If you're in a comfort zone, sometimes it takes a catalyst to snap you into action. When you have a deadline, you can make it happen. If you keep doing the actions that I have outlined here in this book, you will continue to rise. You will continue to grow. You'll reach new heights that maybe you didn't believe were possible.

When you're having success, sometimes it's easy to revert back to your old mindset. You get comfortable. If you feel yourself falling backward, remember you've got goals to reach. Find a new level.

Our program at Strive for 25 helps you find your why, and then figure out how to use that as your anchor. That's your big vision to carry with you. That's how we begin mapping your short-term goals. Your goals are achievable and we can help you get there. When you've got your own "Prosperity Plan"—your own vision board type of mentality—and you're reviewing it every single day, taking the strategies from the book, you're programming your subconscious mind, you'll reach your goals.

If you can look at your plan and do an action every single day on it, you're on your way to building a habit, and if you do even the two minutes a day at first, you'll find yourself excited for your own project.

We want to see you crush it, and reach your goals. The first 30 days are so crucial in starting something new. So we have outlined a process to provide some accountability, but also make it fun.

for the people who want to start a 30 day challenge of jumpstarting a journey toward a new goal, all you have to do is the following:

1) Identify what your high level goal is
2) Identify what near term goal is
3) What is the action item or items you are going to do every single day

4) Send us an email to habits@strivefor25.com every single day that you did your action item

The only way for us to track it is email every single calendar day for 30 straight days.

(needs to be from the same email address every time)

For everyone who successfully completes this process, we will be sending a few strive gear items.

Also, We will hold a drawing every 30 days for a giveaway something of larger value.

If you would like to get in touch, for any other questions, you can email at joel@strivefor25.com.

We look forward to hearing from you, and to watching your financial freedom unfold. Can't wait to see how you will change your life, and those around you!

-Joel Farrell
Strive for 25

Falling off the wagon is inevitable, not a matter if… it's when getting back on track. It's the ability tap into the creativity in our minds to continue to pull out the drive to reach higher levels.